RISKY JOBS

ASTRONAUT

JENNA TOLLI

PowerKiDS press

Published in 2025 by The Rosen Publishing Group, Inc.
2544 Clinton Street, Buffalo, NY 14224

Portions of this work were originally authored by Lissette Gonzalez and published as *Astronauts in Action*. All new material in this edition was authored by Jenna Tolli.

Editor: Jenna Tolli
Book Design: Rachel Rising

Photo Credits: Cover Vadim Sadovski/Shutterstock.com; Cover, pp. 1–24 Apostrophe/Shutterstock.com; Cover, pp. 1–24 ReVelStockArt/Shutterstock.com; Cover, pp. 1–24 Apostrophe/Shutterstock.com; p. 5 https://commons.wikimedia.org/wiki/File:SpaceX_Crew-4_Official_Portrait.jpg; p. 7 Futuras Fotos/Alamy Stock Photo; p. 9 University of College/Shutterstock.com; p. 10 Jose Antonio Perez/Shutterstock.com; p. 11 Everett Collection/Shutterstock.com; p. 13 Dima Zel/Shutterstock.com; p. 14 Vladi333/Shutterstock.com; p. 15 EWY Media/Shutterstock.com; p. 17 LukeandKarla.Travel/Shutterstock.com; p. 18 24K-Production/Shutterstock.com; p. 19 NASA Photo/SAlamy Stock Photo; p. 20 Alones/Shutterstock.com; p. 21 Photo Spirit/Shutterstock.com.

Library of Congress Cataloging-in-Publication Data

Names: Tolli, Jenna, author.
Title: Astronaut / Jenna Tolli.
Description: [Buffalo, New York] : PowerKids Press, [2025] | Series: Risky jobs | Includes bibliographical references and index.
Identifiers: LCCN 2024001090 (print) | LCCN 2024001091 (ebook) | ISBN 9781499446074 (library binding) | ISBN 9781499446067 (paperback) | ISBN 9781499446081 (ebook)
Subjects: LCSH: Astronauts–Juvenile literature. | Manned space flight–Juvenile literature.
Classification: LCC TL793 .T65 2025 (print) | LCC TL793 (ebook) | DDC 629.45–dc23/eng/20240129
LC record available at https://lccn.loc.gov/2024001090
LC ebook record available at https://lccn.loc.gov/2024001091

Manufactured in the United States of America

CPSIA Compliance Information: Batch #CSPK25. For Further Information contact Rosen Publishing at 1-800-237-9932.

CONTENTS

JOURNEY TO SPACE

Space travel is dangerous, or unsafe. Astronauts travel to outer space on **missions** to learn things and explore space. There are lots of different parts of a space mission, and each one has its own risks.

Astronauts in the United States work for NASA. This government organization opens its applications for groups of new astronauts about every four years. Thousands of people apply, but only a small number are chosen. There have only been 360 astronauts since NASA started picking them in 1959. Usually there are between five and seven people on a space mission crew.

DANGER!

Most NASA missions are safe, but three have been deadly. Seventeen astronauts from the United States have died on NASA space missions.

In 2020, over 12,000 people applied to NASA to become an astronaut. Of these, only 10 people were chosen to start training.

HOW TO BECOME AN ASTRONAUT

U.S. citizens can apply to NASA's astronaut candidate training program. To be considered, a person needs to have a college **degree** and have experience in their field. Astronauts have different backgrounds but often study math, science, or engineering. Members of the military can also apply to this training program.

There are health tests to become an astronaut. Working in space is hard and dangerous, so NASA needs to make sure astronauts are healthy and strong enough for the journey. Candidates also need to show that they work well with others. This is important because space crews work as a team.

DANGER!

Astronauts have different jobs in space. Their backgrounds and training help them prepare for these jobs. There are pilots, **commanders**, and **specialists** who handle mission duties.

This shows the first seven American astronauts who went into space, known as the Mercury Seven. You can find profiles of all active and former astronauts on NASA's website.

TRAINING FOR SPACE

Before they go into space, astronauts need to complete a training program that lasts about two years. They learn different skills and information they'll need in space.

In space, gravity changes will make astronauts float and feel weightless. NASA has special training flights on Earth in which planes fly and then dive at certain heights. For about 20 seconds, people on board feel weightless like they will in space.

Another part of this training program is practicing wearing spacesuits underwater. When you float in water, it is similar to how astronauts feel when they float in space!

DANGER!

Spacesuits protect astronauts when they are on space walks. Small objects like space dust can fly at them at very fast speeds, and the suit helps keep them safe.

Astronauts complete their training at NASA's Johnson Space Center, which is in Houston, Texas.

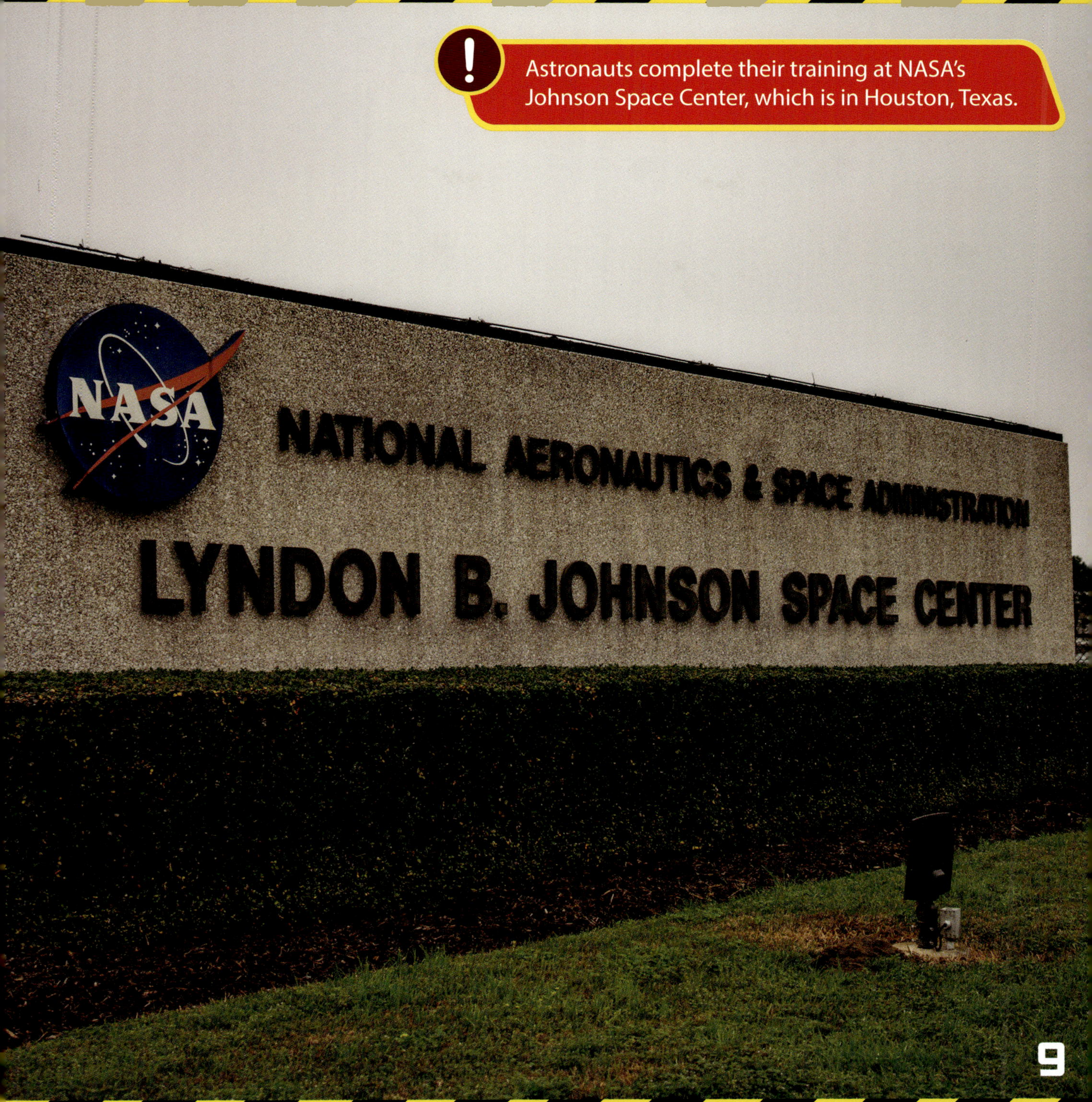

LIFTOFF

Astronauts need to practice every step of a space mission and become **experts** on their spacecraft. From liftoff to landing, they learn to prepare for all kinds of **emergencies**.

When a spacecraft launches, or takes off, from Earth, it is one of the most dangerous and frightening times for an astronaut. In under nine minutes, the spacecraft gets up to 17,500 miles (28,163 km) per hour. It gets very loud inside, and everything shakes. The force of the liftoff makes the astronauts feel a lot of pressure, like something is pressing down on their chest. This can make it hard to breathe.

DANGER!

In 1986, the space shuttle *Challenger* broke apart very quickly after it launched—in just 73 seconds. All seven crew members on board lost their lives.

Astronauts practice for liftoffs during their training. There is more speed, shaking, and noise during a real launch, but lots of the conditions are the same.

RISKS IN SPACE

Being so far away from Earth comes with lots of risks. Medicine, food, and supplies for the journey need to be carefully planned ahead of time. If there is an emergency, it could be very dangerous.

Radiation is one of the most dangerous parts of space travel. You can't see space radiation, but it can be measured with special tools. Too much radiation can lead to serious health problems.

Earth's **atmosphere** protects us from most radiation. When astronauts leave Earth, they aren't protected by the atmosphere anymore. They get exposed to much higher levels of radiation in space.

DANGER!

In the first few days of being in space, astronauts might get dizzy, feel sick, or have headaches. These feelings get better after about a week.

Today, most astronauts go into space to work on the International Space Station (ISS). Astronauts from Europe, Russia, China, Japan, and Canada also work on the ISS.

LANDING

Landing a spacecraft is another very dangerous part of an astronaut's job. Spacecraft travel very fast when they come back to Earth—even faster than the speed of sound! At this high speed, the temperature gets very hot on the outside—up to 3,000°F (1,649°C).

There must be special materials and systems to protect spacecraft from the heat on their way back to Earth. If these systems fail, the spacecraft can get damaged or destroyed due to the temperature. Part of this heat protection system failed on the space shuttle *Columbia*, which caused the last major accident in NASA history.

In 2003, the space shuttle *Columbia* broke apart when it was returning to Earth. The seven crew members were killed. This is a memorial for them.

MISSION CONTROL

From liftoff to landing, astronauts work with a team of people on Earth at NASA's Mission Control Center. This is a team of flight controllers, engineers, **technicians**, and support staff. They oversee the flight, talk to astronauts, and make sure everything is safe. This also includes work on the International Space Station, where astronauts live for months at a time.

The Mission Control Center is responsible for the astronauts' safety and lots of decisions that make space travel possible. These decisions have to be made very fast, especially when they are about safety and how to handle problems.

DANGER!

The phrase, "Houston, we've had a problem," comes from the Apollo 13 mission in 1970. There was a problem on the spacecraft, and astronauts reported this to Mission Control in Houston.

The Mission Control Center is part of NASA's Johnson Space Center in Houston, Texas.

BACK ON EARTH

After astronauts return from a mission, they need time to adjust, or get used, to the changes in gravity. They might experience problems with their muscles, balance, and vision, and changes to their body. The longer an astronaut stays in space, the more challenges they might have when they get back.

NASA keeps track of astronauts' health throughout their lives. They look out for different health risks that astronauts might face and work on ways to make space travel safer for humans. Astronauts are generally healthy after returning from a mission, but many report problems such as back pain in the first few days.

DANGER!

Did you know that astronauts get taller in space? This is related to how gravity affects their spine. They return to their regular height when they get back to Earth.

When they are in space, astronauts need to exercise for about two hours every day. If they don't, they can lose muscle and their bones can get weaker.

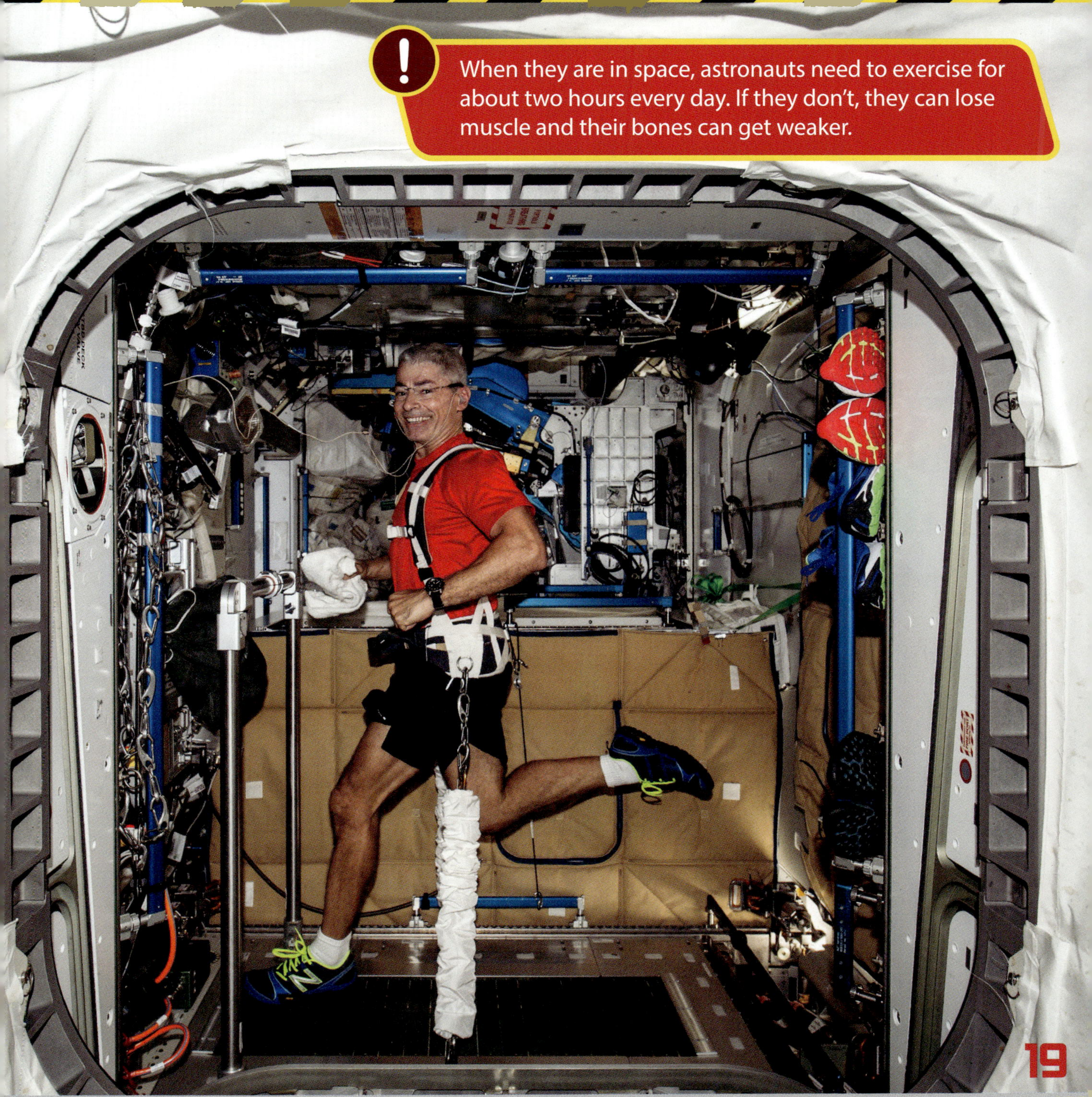

IN THE FUTURE

Astronauts have dangerous jobs, but their work is very important. In space, they study science, **technology**, and other subjects in different ways than we can on Earth. They also use their education and training to stay safe and support themselves in space. NASA is planning new missions and training new astronauts to lead them.

There have been lots of changes in technology since the 1950s, when NASA was founded. Space travel has become safer and more advanced during this time. Even with these advances, astronauts still have one of the most dangerous and exciting jobs in the world.

You can visit NASA's Kennedy Space Center in Florida to learn more about astronauts and space. You could even see a live rocket launch!

GLOSSARY

atmosphere: The mass of air that surrounds Earth or another planet.

commander: A person in an official position of command or control.

degree: A title given to a student by a university or college after completing a program of study.

emergency: An unexpected and usually dangerous situation that calls for immediate action.

expert: Someone who has a special skill or knowledge.

mission: A special job or task.

radiation: Waves of energy that spread outward from something. The sun's light is radiation.

specialist: A person who is an expert in a particular occupation, practice, or field of study.

technician: A person whose work requires special skills.

technology: A method that uses science to solve problems and the tools used to solve those problems.

FOR MORE INFORMATION

BOOKS

Virts, Terry. *The Astronaut's Guide to Leaving the Planet*. New York, NY: Workman Publishing Co., Inc., 2023.

Williams, Dave, and Loredana Cunti. *Go for Liftoff! How to Train Like an Astronaut*. Toronto, Ontario: Annick Press Ltd., 2017.

WEBSITES

Kennedy Space Center
www.kennedyspacecenter.com
Find out more about NASA's Kennedy Space Center in Florida.

Learning Resources for Kids and Students
www.nasa.gov/learning-resources/for-kids-and-students
Learn about NASA, space, and astronauts.

Passport to Space
www.kids.nationalgeographic.com/space
Learn fun facts about planets and exploring space.

Publisher's note to educators and parents: Our editors have carefully reviewed these websites to ensure that they are suitable for students. Many websites change frequently, however, and we cannot guarantee that a site's future contents will continue to meet our high standards of quality and educational value. Be advised that students should be closely supervised whenever they access the internet.

INDEX